# Ghost Beads

Billie Annette

RoseDog✿Books
PITTSBURGH, PENNSYLVANIA 15238

The contents of this work, including, but not limited to, the accuracy of events, people, and places depicted; opinions expressed; permission to use previously published materials included; and any advice given or actions advocated are solely the responsibility of the author, who assumes all liability for said work and indemnifies the publisher against any claims stemming from publication of the work.

Rose Dog Books
585 Alpha Drive
Pittsburgh, PA 15238
Visit our website at www.dorrancebookstore.com

ISBN: 978-1-6461-0304-1
eISBN: 978-1-6464-0373-7

# The Pratt Pack

Not Dean, Sinatra or Sammy
With drinks in hand smiling
Wide mouth teeth gleaming
At some inside joke
Loving life
In the resort casino
Sands
Nope
This was Carlisle
Industrial school
Run by Military Pratt
Eighty two boys and girls in Native dress
Being saved
No smiles here
Lives are about to change
Look it up

# Endings

A tiny baby
Becomes
Lawyer, teacher, doctor
Alcoholic, pan-handler, prostitute
Numbing life someway somehow
Strangers
Separated rooms
But joined together at meals
The teacher forgetting students but loving jello
The lawyer believing he is holding court with his knife gavel
The doctor clutches her doll child protectively
The alcoholic believes nurses are spies
The pan-handler is king being served
The prostitute is afraid of them all
One hopes their lives before held some happiness
No judgement to each
Because
Endings you see
Do not discriminate

# The Children Sleep Lightly At School

The flag yet waved
Before the building of brick and wood
Desk emptied
Because they dared to be
Who and what they remembered
Though fading…
Playground on the right
Cemetery on the left
Keep them sleeping lightly
In their uncomfortable gravely beds
Until they are brought home

# Drive Off

A lazy drive
Beautiful Woman Lake late
Evening is not safe
For them
Or for the little ones asleep in the back
High beams demand stopping
As well as the bumper push
The man exits one
The men exits the other
One armed with emergency bat
And instructions to his wife
That if he goes down
Drive off

# Medicine

He shoos the closet goblins
Ensuring sweet slumber
This time
Her cupping daddy's face
Eases a bruised heart
Little hands
Hold the only medicine

# Empty Pockets

They hold calm
Hiding stress
Fidget a simple paper clip
Clenched hands
Or a key to jangle
Fingers may drum
Secretly
But great wealth
Presented to the one
You bring them empty

# The Pure Time

Soldier boots sink
Into and onto unfamiliar sands
Patent leather
Enters that angry school
Ballet shoe
Challenges strong toe
Formal, tight, shiny
Fits a platform fine
Moccasins
Softly join the circle
Timid, chubby first time foot
For a time prefers no shoe

# Sacred Walk

To recognize abuse
No place for it
Thank you
They trod on the old hill
Where three girls flew
Like juggling props
Off one bike
Crying then laughing
Toboggans flew down it too
It was neighbor
To a yard
That held soft memories
Of skinned knees
Kick the can
Spinning 45's
On the porch
They unknowingly passed
The house that hugged
A family

# After

Then and now
It simply does not
Can not
Fit into the equation
Hopelessness is selfishness
A false nasty root
Dangling aimlessly
Causing confusion
Not being taught
That to rid the disease
Of being selfish
Is to learn
To live
Simply to serve
Make everything
Or anything
Better
For others
Now
And for those
Who will come after

# Thought Path

Yesterday congress agreed
To terminate
Deet those non-humans
The only good one
Is a dead one
Maybe offspring can be molded
Maybe
But why
Ahh
But why not
Today congress agreed
To help
In every way
In any way
It is a great puzzle
Why
Those to be terminated
Have assumed
Oversight
And finish the termination
Themselves

# In-between

Way early
A balanced scale
Simply is
Naive or wise
Child mind
Holds the key to an anger-less world
Way late
A balanced scale may return
To an unblemished mind
Erased by years
A curse or blessing
Egress from whys of mean-ness
Balance between the ways
Is the secret

# Whistle

While fixing a bike chain
During the polishing of black, then brown work shoes
While skimming through the Pioneer
Or perhaps the Star Trib
His lips would purse
Expertly
And that lilt-like sound
Belonging only to him
Found its way to concert ears
Embracing a little girls heart
Hauntingly trying to tell her
She will need to remember
To remember

# Ghost Beads

They are placed by the artist
Once
Per piece
Sometimes strategically
Sometimes not
Either way
They serve as humility reminders
That one cannot create anything
That will be without flaw
This ability remains only with a perfect creator
And we all know
There is only one

# Business as Usual

Mistaken for the Fridge
In his day
Wicked wit
Left benefactors with rolling tears
Faces hurting from laughter
He was pulled over one day
For no other reason
Than odds being in his favor
Or against him
Depending on whose eyes one looked through

# ABC

Gifted
Family loved
Flies away
From rez to prez place
World wind change
Tennis wardrobe
What is that?
Formal dinner dress
Wesley girls
Sniff at her brown presence
Sniffs white stuff
Not for her
This opportunity
A Better Chance

# Gone Library

History cradle
First language survivor
Eyes beholding
Hearts beholding
Minds beholding
Events that may never be known
Are in this treasure chest
An elder dies
A library lost

# Listen

Talking too much
Will allow the wind to muffle
Some kind of empty
Because you weren't given a name
You didn't know you wanted
How does one find it
Ceremony unknown
One can lament
It wasn't given
It wasn't my fault
Really
Listening
Brings what wasn't hidden
It has been there all along
Waiting
You just hadn't heard it yet

# Icing

People
Glamour touches
Unattainable
Ah but so beautiful
Everyone who looks has their favorite
Sultry
Sexy
Perfect teeth
Flat bellies
So flat you can't call them bellies
Shiny hair
Mirror like
Thick, thick, thick
My husband scrapes off icing
And prefers the cake

# Nonchalant

Researching a name
Heard in the wind
She discovered a serial killer
Not pointed out
Like Dahmer
Boston's own
Or the countless others
No concern
Nonchalantly wiki mentions
"Kit sought action and adventure"
Most of us do at some point
Don't we?
Kit found his in killing and scalping
A piece of historic trauma
Falls into place

# Memory Lane

There is one owner
Straight
Curving
Zig-zag like
Happiness lines
Sad ones too
Deep and old
Some just forming
Wrinkles attached to the heart and mind
These are memory lanes
Beauty lines
Adorning the faces
Of us

# Holding Sad

A soldier saluting
Thanking us for thanking him
An owner lying
Next to their dying pet
A loyal pet
Lying on its owners resting place
Shots fired
Ending a generation of tomorrows
Any meanness growing
For no reason other than because it can
A child chooses to bypass hospital
For home then heaven
That thirty something lady
Opting what her death-date will be
Early preparations
So not to burden ones leaving
Wanting to not let go
Of mothers and fathers and children and friends and loved ones who cannot
live forever
Overwhelming sadness
One cannot hold
We never could alone

# New Changes

Faces on every page
Different ages
Thirsty eyes
Promising hopes fill their bellies
As they cross that stage
To make new changes
Fresh eyes
To the table
But what have they witnessed

# Be Beggers

Beg them to tell you
Time and memories
About them and you
Before them and you
Then cradle and document this rare treasure
It will keep you
Beg
Beg
Beg
Hug them
Hold them
Love them
Listen
Listen
Listen
Before they are no more

# Matters

Standing before Mr. Lincoln
My neck hurt trying to see his eyes
The portal to the soul
He did things, I hear
Important matters
Honest man they say
I couldn't say
I couldn't see his eyes

# Treaties

They say they did
Others say they didn't
Others say they did
They say they didn't
Journal
Document
To have a leg to stand on
Drat those pesky written promises

# Morning Companion

Our eyes locked over breakfast
Lean and muscular
Long lashes
Dark mysterious eyes
No give away to thoughts behind them
Frozen stare from me to him
Him to me
Would he frighten easily I wondered
And leave abruptly
Causing me to search
Frantic
Dropping food
Digging in my handbag
Desperate to find a way
To keep him forever with me
But I am too late
He spooks
A white tail vanishes
Deftly
Through the brush

# Actually There are Two

Young
Old
Complicate being
With many paths
Directions vary
When
The basic choice
Is
Good
Or evil

# Acquire Knowledge

Regret nothing
Within reason
If you treasure learning

# Grandfather's Eyes

Fasting
Visions
You laugh
I bristle
Education ends at three
A short rest at the lake
Lonely eagle
Many thoughts
The laughter
Bristles
Peaceful walk home
Talking stomach
Aching unstretched legs
Angry mother asks
What have I done with two days past

# A Real Offer

Be afraid
With me
Not of me
To search the unknown
Treasures
Inside
Outside
Over the moon
Hiding places
That will belong only to us

# "B"

To write
Something about
A friend
So great
Is impossible
So
I'll just call you a Lazy Varmint
And leave it at that

# Blindfold

Knowing what we know
How we can be
If one could create
Cover your eyes
And do it blindly

# Chicken Dumpling Soup for Breakfast

Brain-ache
From words
On the floor
And not saying
What you will find
Around the corner

# Connections

She turned
To find a robin looking at her
Staring
At one another
For a lifetime
Then it flew away
And
She walked back into her office

# Directions

Way left
Sometimes heads nod
Sometimes mine
Way right
Sometimes heads nod
Sometimes mine
Circle into the middle
Its ok then
Its ok now
Probably much later too
But people I fear
Will always scare the bejeezus out of me

# Don't Rush

Running late
Running
Rushing
Short words
Increased mistakes
Hurt
Others
Mostly you

# They Walk Together Now

Silver faces
Now
Smiling lines not familiar to each
Brotherly shove
That cause
Their own smile lines
Now
Memories lie in each
When they kicked rocks
Drew water pistols
Drew blood
Threw attention stones
Gently tick ticking a pane
Fleeing from dads was the fun of it
In that golden duster of yore

# Mean-ness

Cyclone
Anger
Angry
Spit
Internal
Vomit
Will never be my friend

# Here's the Answer

Any boy asks
Always asks
How to treat her
Time and time over
The answer is not known
The centuries old mystery
Given up on many times
Perplexing man
Through the ages
He holds the answer all along
If he only thought
How he would want his mother treated
By his father

# No Other Option

Parents must love
Gently
Kindly
Judiciously
If not
They create scabs
To be left alone

# Silent Hero

How exhausting
To be the first
On many roads
Softening the path alone
Silently struggling
To tie worlds together

# Totally Equal

A new mom
Is asked
By the new dad
What to do
With baby matters
Incredulous
She turns
Asking
How is she to know

# Touch My Soul

Fates choosing
Keeps us apart
I'd wish
Keep in mind
That my heart is on start
For you
To touch my soul

# Not Only Footprints

All are made
By him
Perfect
His fingerprints
Are on us all

# Lone Dancer

It seemed she was
Alone in that circle
Your eyes made it so
She carried the eagle feather
Lifting it to the sky
Her lone dance
Carrying the feather
Now it carry's her

# Original Home

One has no memory
Of it
And can never
Return
To the comfort it holds

# Pennies

Must be from heaven
For now they appear
All the time
As does
Not one
But two
White headed eagles

# Poetry, Poetry

Words
Not only words
Pick your heart
Head
Mind
What you determine them to be
Is
That is the poetry of poetry

# Root

Give to your mother
Be thankful for your father
Receive
Expect nothing
No returns
This will be your strength

# Second Grade Memory

Paints of red and orange
Sponges dipped
Then splooshed on to paper
Creates a landscape
Right before your eyes
Mrs. Nelson created
This most amazing memory

# Uneasy

Soul gnawing
Began at first remembered breakfast
Winds have a picnic
Many this ways
And that ways
One can only dip their toes in so far

# Bridge

A young mother taught
Her children this game
Not of chance
Almost a dance
Of process
Properness
Socially you can fit
Truly you can
Think, plan, play
Etiquette is not bad
Even for the non this or that
Learning trump
A good kind

# The Quiet

Close your eyes
Stillness
Silence
Only then one can hear its sounds
A house settling its bones
An appliance going to work
Whirring
Purring
Ears ringing
But go further
Dig deeper
There is indeed another layer
Hiding even beyond these sounds of silence
A moment or two is all one can hope for
This is the lovely quiet
A gem to be discovered

# Tips to Brow

He walks out
Wearing crisp
The familiar smile
Comfortable gait
To us more than him
Leaving our home
Empty of goodness
Full now of angst
He joins
Us
In the good fight
As I try on
Tips to brow

# Hate Hate

An elderly man glazes
Hoping for a visit
Hungry for anyone
Voice pleasantry
His mind erased
Of his ugly hatred
Of different
Make no mind
If we don't go away young
We will all turn old one day

# I Am Historical Trauma

Amanda
Gina
Michele
I feel for you
Countries feel for you
We all wrap our arms and hearts
Not having the ability to wrap our minds
Around heinous
Knowing time won't heal unseen wounds
But something else might
Ask any tribal nation
We know
Or don't
Know time won't heal unseen wounds
But something else might

# Spacings

Yesterday I would like distance
A touch could burn
Mean could destroy
An untrusting spirit
Was wise at the time
Spacings
No pain
Then you James
Opened and welcomed
At my pace
And allowed me to find
Trust in your space
Now mine

# Hiding Children

Run child
Into the woods
Cover yourself with moss
And sticks
Slow your breathing
Stillness
Listen
Quiet is safety
School will be over soon

# Lessons

It's okay to drink
A sip of courage
The first champagne toast
A can of ballpark
Red antioxidants
Girl's night
Boy's night
Hump night
5 o'clock somewhere spirits
Just learn to not drink
That tall glass of stupid

# Father: A French Fur Trapper Named Josiah

The birth certificate read
The only thread to recognizing
Half family
Half blood
Half history
Half breed
The mirror gave few secrets
To searching hazel eyes
Never discovering
More

# Under

Submerged
Surrounded by cool wet
Feels normal
Buoying
Swishing
Rocking
Outside noises muffle
Thoughts amplify
Know there is magic in the water

# Cannot

One can try to stomach
Pain of lies
Triple six
Somewhere
Theft of 45
Cannot be embraced

# Cardboard Dolls

Don't get involved
Who's business?
Look down and away
Feign sleep
Get over it
Someone else will
Or won't
Count on someone
They had it coming
Not my responsibility
Told you so
Your bed made
Wasn't me
Cardboard dolls cannot be blamed

# Closing Eyes

You can go any
Where
Every
Where
Any
Time
Dads who left
Come back
Moms who left
Come back
Kids who left
Come back
All can move
As freely as they like
If they like
So
I cry
When I hear no one
Dreams they can fly

# Mixed Up

The teacup
Didn't get that way randomly
The almond Hershey
Was planned
His wife
Wasn't German
Her husband
Wasn't Dakota
They got mixed up
I cried again today honey
Honestly
I'm afraid of the mean

# Pomp

They stand a little taller that day
On the final walk of belonging there
In this way
Eyes watch them
Minds remember their turn
Years or decades ago
Recalling
Welcome excited anticipation
Of what comes next
Some know, some don't
Some will; some won't
The square hat with white tassel
Will be moved
Displaying
That if they return
It will always be different

# Honey Gram

This one won't place
Those craving their rightful spot
On her wall of fame
Pitiful her
Pitiful her
Pitiful her
And shame on me
Forgetting
There is only one
In control

# Root Running

Histories entwined
Pulling out the flowers with the weeds
Pulling the flowers and then the weeds
Any way
You still cannot tell which belong to which
Just shake off the mud
And call it family

# Attic Smells

Sneezy dust
Moist soil
Leather musty
A secret odor
Rather kept secret
Lacy linens
Bits of unrecognizable corner stuff
Old books
Rich and richer
Be honest
They transport you somewhere

# Christmas Not Necessary

He gave away gifts
Closing his smiling eyes
They would like these
Well-chosen possessions
Detailed with ribbon
For those he loved
Red ribbons for one
Green ribbons for another
He chose a nylon rope for himself

# Rice Baby

Dimples
Laugh baby
Cry baby
Baby scent
Heaven sent
One step and then another
Trying to make a protective catch
Through a screen
One will accept looking at the treasure
Through glass
Intermittent dreams
Realizing between sighs
That this is all there is
Or can be

# A Trina I Don't Know

Her absence wasn't
Just a person who would not be at the table
There was a story to be learned
Intellect to be sure
Importance of job certainly
Living yes
Mortality everyone
More
The lesson you ask?
Teeter totter

# Unintentional Discovery

Deep enough
A gem here
Bones there
Digging holes
Pull back sashes
Finding
False friends
And true enemies

# No More Borders

Every weekend he went home
From teaching to being taught
Pathways made by him alone
Canadian air
Fills his lungs
Moss and leaves embrace
As he crossed the final border

# Peanuts

His favorite color blue
Her rose tattoo
Sealing any deal
Really real
From bottom to top
A journey with no stop
Smiling through back pain both
Still throwing away peanut shells

# Putting On the Rose

You can laugh at broken bridges
When stepping across
Frozen waves

# Want to Talk With My Mom

Only their absence scared her
Alone minus the goslings
Who never questions
Or had to
Their safe passage
Behind her
Stop talking
And listen

# Fresh Bread

The big knife slices
Souls
Curiously adorns
Silver
Shiny buttons
A side arm
Slight swing
Soldier march
As long as it stays
In leather
We are good to shake hands

# Right Now

Be strong enough
To see out
Seek out
Lasting change
Impact
To taste color
Feel reds
Or yellows
Do

# Happen

Real dangers
Changers
In charge
Charges through
He and you
Ruining
Running
Smirking green devil
Devil, devil
One prays for you
Through concrete cement

# Beckoning

Tiny twirler
May call out
Teen twister
Glances at stove
And the pillar standing there
Laced lady
Won't start until her presence
Choked heart
Wondering how
Can good keep
Without seeing
Those hands on hips

# Eventually

History forts
Built to keep safe
From whom or what
Safe were those outside
Safe were those inside
Wooden remnants
Snow forts always melt

# Her Brain Cries Alone

Turning final pages
Reading last words
No more new
Anticipation dissipated
Knowing the end
Small books close too
With a name erased
But not the story

# Murky

Below the deep
One just cannot know
Can
Not
Know
Choose not to step
In angry waters

# Country Aches

There was no way it could be
Having jumped from cracked counters
Yelling spit
To sparkling waters
Unable to assess lips
Touching silver
We now move
To counting sand

# A Montana Cabin Anywhere

No mother may I needed
Leaving wonder behind
Solitude from untruths
Crushing unknowns
Crashing waves beckon
Throwing back and forth realness
He stepped off that plan
To their never again

# Hiding History

Peeking in covered windows
At ruined children
Wonders of why
Playing yesterday
Running today
Rattling cages forever
Eventually it will be know
Second helpings of hidden history

# Wine Ties Lies

Toasts
The yellow house
Events
Privacy fence
To keep away
Prying eyes
Wine ties lies
Evaporating
All
Toasts

# Souls We Keep

The turtle was crossing
Then escaped into itself
Like all do at times
Auto slows
To a crawl
Too slow a crawl
The world looked safe again
The driver felt the thump
That lasts a lifetime

# Not Korn

That sound
More than a wail
Growling ache
Low gravelly pain
Citizen deity dead
No uncle tom here
All they knew
All that was written
Burned
Branded
Minds
It's time to burn books
Start over

# Adam's Edge

Following the edge of a brim
With a nervous finger helps
The edge of night
Whispers dawn
Edge of a seat
Provides quicker flight
Edge of paper
May border thoughts
Momentarily
Adam's edge
Nervously hoped for dawn
Leaving no bordered thoughts
He stepped over

# Boxes

Quietly her mind said no
All those years ago
No one would know
Or even care
Her strength would come to bare
A steely stare
Efficient are
Boxes for this and that

# My Ford

She ran on intellect
Soft soul interior
Ethos eyes
Her plea was belief
Unnecessary confirmation
From anyone
Stating aloud
To the world
Would shed his stink
For others too
Sister strangers
That lay sleeping

# Ant

They work
Oblivious
Working, working
To what end I wonder
A foot may sweep all away
Crushing homes
Burying family
Water destroying
Washing away existence
Who knows if there is sorrow
Anger
Perhaps
Sometimes notices
Most times no
Maybe we are ants

# We Live

Much runs through veins
Yesterday's everything
From hundreds of years
Carried into tomorrow
To hundreds of years
We learn to peek around
Broken blood
Than cannot be stitched
To fix unbroken

# Borrowing

Great hunters framed
A proud dad and his sons
Deer stretched out
Success for each
Stories would be told
The hunt
The kill
The eldest son
A dad's hunting story
Would not be told
Until years later
Even with a clear
Perfect shot
He could not
Would not
Pull the trigger
Pulling me closer
To knowing him
Him

# Park House

She storied tales
Buttoning and unbuttoning her grand dress pajama
Smoothing out her coiffed unruly gray mane
To no one listening
What an incorrigible boy David was
Playing pranks
Sliding down the majestic banister
Wanda scolded
The rascally imp
Feigning exasperation
She tidied shiny golden hair
Reflected back to the young lady
In the ornate wall mirror
Where
A rug softened the legs
Of baby grand
Now she clings to her doll
While her son feeds her soup

# Two Windows

I sit upon blue flowers
Winding white on the quilt-like coverlet
Staring out one window
Facing the gravel alley
My feet knew well
I shall see it only a bit longer
A wafting breeze
Moves the thin curtains
Caressing my face
A momentary visitor
That will escape out the other window
Leaving behind
A life we all eventually miss

# Finding Safe

You won't know it
Until you know it
Nothing to qualify
Authentic peace
Old clothes
New suits
You may choose
Smiling inside and out
Because it truly won't matter

# <u>Yet</u>

Sleigh
Float on fresh white
Merry
Go round and round
Spin cool dizzy endless
Hope
Not needed yet
When you
Absolutely are unable to hate